Reply cards & env

You can include an address for people to reply to, but a good way to elicit a quick response is to include a card that can be completed and posted back to you. If your budget permits, you could also include a stamped, self-addressed envelope, and then they've got no excuse!

Small reply cards, printed with the invitations, can be worded so that all your friends and family need to do is delete the appropriate word or words.

Example
> I/We would love to attend/will be unable to attend
> the wedding of [bride and groom] on...

There could also be options for:
- selecting a vegetarian or vegan option
- specifying the total number of family members who will be attending
- (for a marriage or christening) stating whether the guest will be attending both the service and the party/ reception afterwards.

Personalised stationery ranges, such as those available at Confetti, include coordinated reply cards.

It's a good idea to add a date by when you would like to receive replies. Remember to give yourself plenty of time to ask other people if you find you've got space to fill. A sensible date is one or two months before the event, or whatever makes sense for your arrangements. After this date, start ringing round any stragglers to receive their answers.

Example

....

is/are pleased to accept your kind
invitation to the marriage of your
daughter [bride's first names] to
Mr [groom's first names and surname]
on [day and date]

Or

M...

will ...... attend
The favour of a reply is requested
before [date]

Or

M...

.... will attend
...........................will not attend
The favour of a reply is requested
before [date]

Whatever you do, whenever you include the letters RSVP (*répondez s'il vous plaît*), make sure you include an address, email address or phone number for guests to reply to.

Choosing a theme

The first thing you need to do when sending out any kind of invitation is to consider your theme. This needn't be as detailed as 'Elvis in Hawaii' or 'Guys and Dolls', but simply means the kind of atmosphere you want your invitations to convey, as this is the first glimpse your guests will have of the tone of your event.

Plain invitations on a white or ivory background, with black embossed or engraved ink in a cursive font, will immediately suggest a very formal event and give the guest very few clues beyond that. However, if you choose a different kind of invitation, the guests may be able to take their cue from both the style and the colour of the invitation.

Invitation colour
It has become the custom nowadays to colour-coordinate most events, especially weddings and anniversaries. So if you have decided on blue and white flowers or table decorations at your event, it is natural to choose a blue and white invitation, perhaps accessorized with blue ink – or even silver.

Invitation style
Celtic, modernist, minimalist, floral, oriental, funky, traditional, chic – whatever the tone of your event, there is an invitation design to suit your needs.

Once you have chosen the theme of your stationery you can continue the same design throughout your event with, for instance, tableware that will perfectly match the style of your invitations and can add a sense of sophistication to your celebrations.

Menus

Menu cards may be printed for your guests but you should not feel obliged to provide them; this should be a budget decision as they can be expensive. At home, these can be made by hand, or a hotel or restaurant may provide them as a matter of course.

Place or name cards

If you are having pre-arranged seating, place cards (sometimes called name cards) are a useful way of letting guests know where to sit. If you put the names on both sides, they also make a tactful *aide-mémoire* for guests who have just met each other! You can have them professionally printed, design them yourself on a computer, or simply write them with a calligraphy pen. If your invitations were addressed formally, you should use the same formality on your place cards. If the invitation said 'Jane', then so should the place card, but if you addressed the invitation to Mrs Jane Eccles, then this is the correct form for the place card.

Seating plans

In addition to place cards, for large gatherings an overall seating plan is usually prepared so that guests know the general location of their seats as they enter the dining room.

It is also a lovely idea to write a little personalized note inside each place card to welcome your guests. A short sentiment such as 'Thank you for coming!' or 'Hope you'll join us on the dance floor!' is all that is needed.

Favour boxes

The long-standing tradition of giving bomboniere to celebrate special occasions such as weddings was started centuries ago in Italy. Each traditionally contains five top-quality sugared almonds, as five is a prime number that cannot be divided, just like the bride and groom, and symbolizing health, wealth, happiness, fertility and a long life. These little gifts are now also cropping up at corporate parties, birthdays, anniversaries and even formal dinners at home. Put at place settings, they make a wonderful way of saying thank you to your guests.

Cake boxes & bags

Small boxes with greaseproof inner linings for sending portions of wedding cake to those guests unable to attend are another stationery option. These can be personalized and made to match your overall theme, and you can also include a 'with compliments' card to dispatch with the cake. Bags can be provided for those guests at the reception who prefer to take their piece of cake home.

Guest cards

If you are holding a particularly complex event, such as a
wedding abroad or an anniversary weekend, you may also
want to use guest cards. These simply give an outline of
proceedings so guests know where they ought to be and
when. They can be laid out rather like a menu, with the
'courses' being the days, or even 'ceremony', 'wedding
breakfast', 'evening reception', and so on.

Other items

Don't go thinking this is the end of the list… There are
still monogrammed napkins, napkin rings, drink mats and
matchbooks to be considered. Then there are the more
unusual items such as pre-printed ribbon, balloons,
personalized confetti and bottle labels. Selecting a few of
these can be a simple way to create a coordinated look —
and, of course, they make great mementos!

Wedding stationery

For many people, organizing their wedding means they are suddenly launched into a perplexing world of stationery etiquette. What should they send to whom? How should invitations be phrased? And, of course, there is always the worry that you might commit some breach of etiquette that will mortally offend Great Aunt Ethel, who's been to 87 weddings and is a stickler for doing things in the proper way!

Actually, wedding stationery is a lot simpler than it first appears. Although there seem to be a lot of different items, each one, in fact, communicates something specific to your guests. The appropriate one to choose will therefore come naturally to you, depending on the kind of wedding you are having. Planning on an intimate wedding breakfast followed by a huge knees up with all your family and friends? Then you'll want wedding invitations and evening invitations. A hearty church service with lots of hymns? Then you'll want an Order of Service to make sure your guests all sing the same words. Read on for plenty of advice on choosing your stationery, as well as on the correct wording for every occasion.

Before the wedding

Engagement announcements

As an engaged couple, you'll be keen to tell as many
relatives and friends as possible your good news.
Compile a list and then decide whether you wish to
inform them by visit, letter, telephone, email or at a
celebratory party. If you want to make an additional,
more formal announcement, it's traditional for the
bride's parents to announce the news in a local or
national newspaper.

Of course, the hippest couples announce their
engagement on the internet, so that friends
and family online around the world can access
the announcement and see pictures of the
couple together.

All users of confetti.co.uk can set up their own
personal wedding web pages. To register, log on to
www.confetti.co.uk

Formal wording

Formal notification can be sent out on personalized or monogrammed notepaper. If you do not have this, you can just print the bride-to-be's parents' names at the bottom.

Example

We are delighted to announce the engagement of
our daughter Felicity Jane to Mark Edward,
son of Mr and Mrs Anthony Shaw of Kingsbridge, Devon.

Informal wording

Nowadays, most couples simply tell their family, friends, work colleagues and passing strangers about their engagement by email, phone or word of mouth. This is perfectly acceptable. Avoid sending out engagement announcements to those whom you know you will not invite to the wedding.

Invitations to an engagement party

Traditionally, the bride's parents would host the engagement party, and if this was not possible, the groom's parents would step in. Friends of the family might also offer to host the party, and in this case the invitations should be sent from them. Nowadays, anything goes and many couples, particularly those who have lived together before deciding to get married, will host their own engagement party.

Invitations should say that the party is held 'in honour' of you and your fiancé. They do not have to mention that the event is to be held in celebration of your engagement, as this is generally a given.

You may wish to announce your engagement at the party. If so, neither your name nor your fiancé's should appear on the invitations, as this will give away the surprise!

Example

Mr and Mrs [bride's parents' name]
request the pleasure of your company
at a dinner in honour of
Miss [bride's name] and Mr [groom's name]
on [day and date]
at [time]
at [venue + full address]
RSVP

Or

Miss [bride's name] and Mr [groom's name]
request the pleasure of your company
at a party in their honour
on [day and date]
at [time]
at [venue + full address]
RSVP

Invitations to a 'meeting you' party

For couples who have just got engaged but whose parents have yet to meet, a 'meeting you' party may be in order.

The 'meeting you' party is often held instead of an engagement party, though some couples hold both.

Example

Invitation
To meet Miss [bride's name]

Mr and Mrs [groom's parents' name]
request the pleasure of your company
at a cocktail reception
on [day and date]
at [time]
at [venue + full address]
RSVP

Hen and stag invitations

The 'last night of freedom!' Inviting friends and family to your hen or stag do can be less formal – in fact, this really is a case of anything goes!

Hen and stag parties are typically organized by the chief bridesmaid or the best man. Whether you are organizing your own 'last night of freedom' or doing it for a friend, it is important to make sure that those invited are given all the relevant information. As hen and stag dos are usually paid for by each guest, you might even want to give instructions as to how much money each person should pay and who this should be given to.

Example

Last night of freedom!
Send [bride's name] off in style
on [day and date]
at [venue + full address]
from [time] till late…
RSVP
Entry to the club has been prepaid. Please make cheques for £15 payable to Pauline Murray. Thanks.

Or

For an evening of eating, drinking
and ritual humiliation...
[groom's name]
requests the pleasure of your company
at his stag night
on [day and date]
at [time]
at [venue + full address]
RSVP

Or

See me on my way to extreme wedded bliss!
[groom's name]
is having a stag night
on [day and date]
at [time]
at [venue + full address]
RSVP

Or

No 'L' plates, please…
…but I wouldn't say no to a drink!
[bride's name]
is having her hen night
on [day and date]
at [time]
at [venue + full address]
RSVP

Or

Bring your incriminating photos and embarrassing stories
and we'll bring the blushing bride!
Please help send [bride's name] off in style
on [day and date]
at [time]
at [venue + full address]
RSVP

Invitations to a bridal shower

The bridal shower is a lovely old American tradition: a time for friends and family to shower the bride and groom with gifts for their future lives together. The bridal shower may take the place of the wedding list, providing the opportunity for friends and family to give the bride and groom everything they'll need for their new home together.

Bridal showers are usually hosted by the bride's friends, and the invitations can be informal. They often have gift themes to guide the guests, such as linens or garden equipment and kitchenware: this should be mentioned on the invitation, preferably in the lower right-hand corner.

Brides who have been married before rarely have a shower the second time around, mainly because they are likely already to have everything they need for their home. It would nevertheless be appropriate to host a shower for a bride who did not have one the first time round.

It should be noted that it is deemed inappropriate for the bride's family to host the bridal shower, as this could be seen as the bride's family soliciting gifts on her behalf!

Example

[Host's first name and surname]
requests the pleasure of your company
at the bridal shower
in honour of
[bride's first name and surname]
on [day and date]
at [time]
at [venue + full address]
RSVP [contact details]

Garden and kitchenware

Or

[Multiple friend's first names and surnames]
invites you to a surprise bridal shower
in honour of
[bride's first name and surname]
on [day and date]
at [time]
at [venue + full address]

Please reply to
[friend's first name and surname] on [phone no.]

Linens

Invitations to a rehearsal dinner

The wedding rehearsal is generally held a few days before the wedding and is simply an opportunity to run through the words and moves for the big day. It is customary for the groom's parents to host a rehearsal dinner on the night before the wedding, as a courtesy to the bride's parents, who host the wedding. Invitations to the rehearsal dinner are usually formal, but should be used as a guide to how the bride, groom and their parents would like to be addressed.

While the rehearsal dinner should not compete with the wedding, it is usual for the invitations to complement the wedding invitations (but not to match them).

Usually it is just the bridal party that is invited to the rehearsal dinner but anyone else can be invited as well. Invitations should be sent two weeks before the wedding.

Example

Mr and Mrs [groom's parents' name]
request the pleasure of your company
at a rehearsal dinner
in honour of
Miss [bride's first name and surname]
and
Mr [groom's first name and surname]
on [day and date]
at [time]
at [venue + full address]
RSVP

Or

[Groom's parents' first name]
request the pleasure of your company
at a rehearsal dinner
in honour of
[bride's first name] and [groom's first name]
on [day and date]
at [time]
at [venue + full address]
RSVP

Save the Date cards

These are a great way of announcing your wedding date to guests in advance of your invitations, to ensure that they keep the date free. Particularly useful for summer weddings (when guests may wish to book their holidays) and for overseas weddings or guests, these cards help to ensure that no one misses your special day.

They are usually sent out around three to six months before the wedding, though they can be sent as early as a year in advance. They should match the wedding invitations that follow, and should ideally take the form of small invitations sent in an envelope.

Remember that for everyone to whom you send a Save the Date card, make sure that they are on your final guest list, as once you have asked them to book the weekend, you can't uninvite them!

Example

Please save the date of
Friday 10th August, 2005
for the wedding of
Miss [bride's name]
to
Mr [groom's name]

Mr and Mrs [bride's parents' name]

The wedding

Your wedding invitations will set the tone for the wedding, and should therefore reflect the style and level of formality of the day. The style you choose is simply a matter of taste. Traditional weddings call for formal invitations, whereas smaller civil weddings can get away with a more modern style. For themed weddings, invitations can be made in keeping with the theme: for instance, a Tudor themed wedding would be complemented by a 16th-century-style invitation, complete with a scroll font on parchment.

Your wedding stationery can be obtained from a number of sources: mail order, a printer, stationer and stationery designers, or you can buy online from Confetti, with its own extensive range of wedding stationery.

The range of alternatives and styles of wedding invitation is vast, and it would be all too easy to get carried away. You may expect that you will simply choose the invitation style you want, and that it will be printed and supplied with matching envelopes – and you are away. Certainly in some cases this may be so, but wait until you see the huge range on offer:

INVITATIONS REPLY CARDS ENVELOPE SEALS

CAKE BOXES PLACE CARDS ORDER OF SERVICE SHEETS

MATCHBOOKS NAPKINS NAPKIN RINGS

COASTERS BRIDAL FAVOUR BOXES

GUEST SCROLLS MENUS THANK-YOU CARDS

GUEST AUTOGRAPH ALBUM ADHESIVE BOTTLE LABELS

PERSONALIZED RIBBON... you can even have

AFTER-DINNER MINTS WITH PERSONALIZED WRAPPERS!

For more details on these, see pages 13–19.

Remember that you will almost certainly be working to a budget, and nice as some of these items are, you need to know where to draw the line. It would be all too easy to go overboard and spend a fortune that could perhaps have been better spent elsewhere. However, it should also be said that many of these items make delightful keepsakes, and at least some are worth considering. They can also provide a wonderful way of continuing the theme of your wedding.

You will need to order the invitations at least three months in advance, or as soon as you have a good idea of numbers.

You should allow one invitation per family, including courtesy ones for the groom's parents and the minister and his or her partner. Also include family and friends whom you may already know cannot come but who would appreciate receiving an invitation, for example, a very elderly grandparent.

Don't forget to order a spare 20 or so invitations to allow for mistakes when writing them, and for any extra guests you may decide to ask at a later date.

Create your own stationery

There are two basic types of 'make your own' stationery.

The first involves purchasing invitations, reply cards, etc, preprinted with a design but blank inside. You can then purchase either blank inserts or inserts that are laid out as follows:

Example

....

request the pleasure of the company of

....

at the marriage of

....

to

....

on..............................

at..............................

at..............................

The blank inserts can be used to print your own invitations on a home PC, and the pre-formatted ones simply need the gaps filled in (in your best handwriting or calligraphy).

The second way of making your own stationery involves creating the design yourself. Plain, blank cards, envelopes and inserts in a variety of colours are widely available, including at www.confetti.co.uk. It's entirely up to you how you decorate them; perhaps with a printed photograph or caricature, or with a more abstract design. Here are some ideas for trimmings:

Paper confetti
Fabric confetti
Paper flowers
Sweets such as love hearts
Feathers
Ribbon
Paper butterflies
Little glass or plastic jewels
Paper stars

For more ideas and a large range of trimmings, visit www.confetti.co.uk

Personalized stationery

'Personalized stationery' means stationery that is created just for you from a basic design. Preprinted with the wording of your choice, it is the traditional choice for wedding invitations and coordinating stationery.

Personalization is available on everything from place cards to orders of service, and good suppliers will allow you to choose your typeface, your occasion and even your language.

When ordering personalized stationery, it is important to keep records of everything you have sent to your printer: this isn't in case you discover any errors, it's in case the printer makes mistakes and you can prove it was them and not you. Some stationery services, including Confetti, allow you to submit your wording online, which removes much of the room for error. See www.confetti.co.uk/invitations for more information.

Formal wedding invitations are engraved in black ink, usually on white or ecru-coloured card. They should be in 'letter sheet', which means they will have a fold on the left-hand side and open like a book.

The choice of typeface is yours, although script styles tend to look more formal. Script styles should not be placed within a border. Invitations can be any size, though traditionally they are 6 x 8in, 5 x 7in or 4 x 6in. The larger sizes may be folded again across the centre. Whatever their size, they should fit into matching envelopes.

Always ask your printer to provide you with proofs before the invitations are printed. This way any tiny spelling or layout mistakes can be corrected easily and your invitations will go out perfect.

For more informal wedding invitations, anything goes, and these days it is perfectly acceptable to send out invitations featuring caricatures of the happy couple. The choice of colour, size and font is up to you.

Invitations to the wedding and wedding breakfast should be sent as soon as the venues are booked. It is usual to send them out about eight to twelve weeks before the wedding, but the earlier the better.

The invitation should include a response date by which time acceptances should be received, ideally no later than four weeks before the wedding. Once these acceptances have been received, you will be in a better position to send out the evening invitations. If the reception venue you have booked requires you to seat a minimum number of guests, then you can extend a day invitation to evening guests if some guests are unable to make it.

Bear in mind when phrasing your invitations that equal line lengths generally look better on the page than an array of different line lengths. Quite apart from the information it contains, you want the invitation to look good.

The wording may vary according to taste, but whatever the format, the invitation should state the following:
- names of the bride's parents or other hosts
- first name of the bride
- first name and surname of the bridegroom and his title (Mr/Lieutenant/Sir)
- where the ceremony is taking place
- date, month and year of the wedding ceremony
- time of the ceremony
- location of the wedding reception
- address to which guests must reply

Invitations always go out from whoever is hosting the wedding – usually the bride's parents. The wording gets more complicated if parents are divorced, or if the couple are hosting the event themselves. The usual wording for a traditional invitation is:

Example

Mr and Mrs James Jones
request the pleasure of your company
(or request the honour of your presence)
at the marriage of their daughter
Susan
to Mr Neil Wood
on [day + date]
at [time]
at [venue + full address]
RSVP [hosts' address]

Who does an invitation invite?

Invitations should always be addressed to the people you want to attend your wedding: 'Margaret, Michael and family' would suggest all the children are invited, for example. 'Margaret and Michael' clearly means Margaret and Michael alone. 'Margaret, Michael and Fiona' again means just what it says. Anyone who then turns up with the full family in tow is being blatantly bad mannered.

Deciding not to have children at your wedding can be difficult, but not half as tough as informing their parents! You should let people know as early as possible if their children are not invited, to give them plenty of time to organize childcare.

In theory, if a child's name is not included on the invitation, the parents should realize that he or she is not invited. But, in practice, some people – particularly new parents – will just assume they can bring their little darlings with them. So to avoid any misunderstandings, be clear from the outset.

There are several ways of letting people know their children are not invited. The first is to tell parents tactfully before the invitations go out. Enlist your own parents and close friends to help you spread the word, and have an explanation ready. Perhaps you've decided not to invite children because it will be a long day culminating in a late evening, or because the venue does not allow children, or because you know so many little ones that limited space or costs means you can't include them all, and it would be unfair to include only some.

If you are blushing at the thought of broaching the subject in person, do it in writing. However, printing 'no children' on the invitations is not an option. It's not exactly courteous and will only cause offence. Instead, try something along these lines: 'We regret that we are unable to cater/provide facilities for children.'

Alternatively, you could mention it in your information pack (see pages 68–70), with a single sentence saying: 'We are sorry that we are unable to invite babies and children to the wedding.' Not only does this make the situation clear, but it also implies that your decision is due to circumstances beyond your control.

Examples of wedding invitations

The bride's parents

Mr & Mrs Wakefield
request the honour of your presence
at the marriage of their daughter
Laura-Jayne Elizabeth
to Adam Steven Austin
on [day, month, year]
at [time]
at
St George's Church, Barton-in-Fabis,
Nottingham

Both sets of parents

Mr & Mrs Wakefield
and
Mr & Mrs Austin
request the pleasure of your company
at the marriage of
Laura-Jayne Elizabeth
to Adam Steven Austin
on [day, month, year]
at [time]
at
St George's Church, Barton-in-Fabis,
Nottingham

You're hosting your own

Ms Laura-Jayne Elizabeth Wakefield
and
Mr Adam Steven Austin
request the pleasure of your company
at their marriage
on [day, month, year]
at [time]
at
St George's Church, Barton-in-Fabis,
Nottingham

You with both sets of parents

Mr & Mrs Wakefield
and their daughter
Laura-Jayne Elizabeth
together with
Mr & Mrs Austin
and their son
Adam Steven Austin
request the honour of your presence
at the wedding of
Laura-Jayne Elizabeth
and
Adam Steven
on [day, month, year]
at [time]
at
St George's Church, Barton-in-Fabis,
Nottingham

Single parent

Mr Wakefield
requests the honour of your presence
at the marriage of his daughter
Laura-Jayne Elizabeth
to
Adam Steven Austin
on [day, month, year]
at [time]
at
St George's Church, Barton-in-Fabis,
Nottingham

Divorced parent with spouse/bride or groom's step-parent

Jane & Tom Brown
request the pleasure of your company
at the marriage of Jane Brown's daughter
Laura-Jayne Elizabeth Wakefield
to
Adam Steven Austin
on [day, month, year]
at [time]
at
St George's Church, Barton-in-Fabis,
Nottingham

Jointly hosted by divorced parents

Example

Mr Wakefield

and

Mrs Brown

request the pleasure of your company

at the marriage of their daughter

Laura-Jayne Elizabeth Wakefield

to

Adam Steven Austin

on [day, month, year]

at [time]

at

St George's Church, Barton-in-Fabis,

Nottingham

Someone other than the bride's parents

If the host of the wedding is not a parent of either the bride or the groom but another relation, you should word the invitation accordingly, adjusting the word 'daughter/son' and adding the hosts' relationship.

- Grandparents = granddaughter/grandson
- Aunt and uncle = niece/nephew
- Godparents = goddaughter/godson
- Foster parents = foster daughter/foster son
- Brother = sister/brother
- Sister = sister/brother

Other alternatives

You may want to leave room for the guest's name in the text, rather than at the top of the invitation. This would read as follows:

Mr and Mrs Francis Black
request the pleasure of the company of
....
at the marriage of their daughter
Laura-Jayne Elizabeth Wakefield
to
Adam Steven Austin

Double wedding

If two daughters are being married on the same day, the elder is listed first.

Nuptial mass

Catholics marrying at a nuptial mass may like to use the following phrase in their invitation:

Mr and Mrs Francis Black
request the honour of your company

Although it is traditional to simply invite people to the wedding and not mention the venue for the reception afterwards, you may want to add a few words on the end of your invitation such as, 'and afterwards at a reception at (venue)' in order to clarify that you would like them to attend.

The wording can also be adapted to accommodate changes of circumstances owing to death, divorce or remarriage on the bride's side.

If either parent is widowed:
'Mr James Jones/Mrs Pamela Jones, requests the pleasure'

If parents are divorced:
'Mr James Jones and Mrs Pamela Jones request the pleasure'

If parents are divorced and the mother has remarried:
'Mr James Jones and Mrs Pamela Matthews'

Continental Europeans and members of the practising Jewish community send cards including the names of both sets of parents. Jewish invitations say 'and' rather than 'to', reflecting the belief that two families are being united, rather than that the bride is being given away.

Example

Mr & Mrs Paul Goldberg
request the honour of your presence
at the marriage of their daughter
Laura-Jayne Elizabeth
and
Adam Steven
son of
Mr & Mrs Mitchell Stein
on [day, month, year]
at [time]
at
Sinai Synagogue, Roman Avenue, Leeds

Or

Mr & Mrs Paul Goldberg &
Mr & Mrs Mitchell Stein
request the honour of your presence at the marriage of
Laura-Jayne Elizabeth Goldberg
and
Adam Steven Stein
on [day, month, year]
at [time]
at
Sinai Synagogue, Roman Avenue, Leeds

Reception only

If the ceremony venue is limited in size, it may be a good idea to send reception invitations to all, and an additional ceremony invitation to those guests invited to both.

Reception invitations should 'request the pleasure of your company', and it is equally correct to call it a marriage reception or a wedding reception, though the latter is more common.

Example (ceremony card)

The honour of your presence is requested
at the marriage ceremony
on [day and date]
at [time]
at [venue + full address]

Example (reception card)

The honour of your presence is requested
at the wedding reception
on [day and date]
at [time]
at [venue + full address]

Admission cards

These are generally only used by well-known people, who may want to take every precaution to deter gatecrashers. The admission card acts like an entry ticket, may be sent with the wedding invitations and should be personalised to avoid misuse.

Example

Mr Geoffrey Pithers
PLEASE PRESENT THIS CARD
at St Michael's Church
on Monday, 5th May, 2004

Or

Mr Geoffrey Pithers
Christ Church
Ceremony at eight o'clock
Present card at door

Late receptions

Receptions held after the day of the wedding ceremony, are becoming increasingly popular, especially for those getting married abroad.

A reception that is held after the day of the wedding should not be referred to as a wedding reception, but rather as a party or reception held in honour of the recently married couple.

Late receptions are ideal for families and friends of the bride and groom who live a long distance away. Late reception invitations should read 'in honour of'.

Example

Mr and Mrs [bride's parents' names]
request the pleasure of your company
at a dinner reception
in honour of
Mr and Mrs [bride and groom's names]
on [day and date]
at [time]
at [venue + full address]

For other reception and ceremony stationery, see pages 13–19.

Invitations to the evening reception

These are usually sent out after the responses to the day invitations have been received.

Example

Mr and Mrs [bride's parents' name]
request the pleasure of your company
at an evening reception
to celebrate the marriage of their daughter
[bride's name]
to
Mr [groom's name]
on [day and date]
at [time]
at [venue + full address]

Inviting evening guests to the ceremony

You may wish to let evening guests know that they are also welcome at the ceremony. If your invitation is very formal in style and tone, it is best to include a line to this effect in your information pack (see pages 68–70) or enclose a separate note. If your invitation is less formal, you could simply add a line at the bottom saying: 'You are very welcome at the ceremony at [time] [venue].

Invitations to a wedding abroad

These can be worded in much the same way as a domestic wedding invitation, but you will need to send them out much earlier.

Alternatively, you can send out a Save the Date card and an information pack (see pages 35 & 68–70 for more details) in advance, and then send the invitations out, as a formality, six to twelve weeks in advance.

Postponing a wedding

Your wedding may have to be postponed for a number
of reasons. With luck, this is not something you'll have
to worry about, but if the situation should arise, you need
to inform your guests of the fact, and to do so just as
formally as you invited them.

Postponement and cancellation announcements require
the host to recall their wedding invitations.

In the case of a postponement, a new invitation can
then be issued.

Recalling wedding invitations

When a wedding is postponed, the invitations should
be recalled, to be replaced by new ones. Recalling the
invitations will officially cancel them so that a new date
can be set. The reason for the postponement should be
mentioned on the recall notice, which should match both
the original wedding invitation and the new invitation.
When the wedding is postponed at short notice, it is
acceptable to notify guests by phone.

Example

Mr and Mrs [bride's parents' names]
regret that the illness of their daughter
[bride's name]
obliges them to recall their invitation to her marriage to
Mr [groom's name]
on [day and date]

New invitation

Example

Mr and Mrs [bride's parents' names]
announce that the wedding of their daughter
Miss [bride's name]
to
Mr [groom's name],
which was postponed, will now take place
on [day and date]
at [time]
at [venue + full address]

Cancelling a wedding

If you decide to call off your wedding, telling everyone is probably the last thing you want to do. The best way to do it is with a simple note to all your guests. You don't have to go into detail, just a basic 'Janet and John regret to inform you that the wedding arranged for (date, time, venue) will not now take place' will do. If you wish, you can add a personal note, such as, 'We'd like to thank you for all your good wishes in the past.'

Formal notification cards should match the invitations and should be sent as soon as possible. If the wedding is cancelled at short notice, it is advisable to make the announcement by phone.

Example

Mr and Mrs [bride's parents' names]
are obliged to recall their invitation
to the marriage of their daughter
[bride's name]
to
Mr [groom's name]
as the marriage will not be taking place

To enclose or not to enclose?

For the sake of convenience, you may wish to include details of your gift list with your invitation – just bear in mind that this isn't the traditional approach. Your older guests will be more familiar with the idea of asking the bride's mother for details once the invitations have been issued.

Most companies that offer a wedding gift list service will provide you with a printed card with all the relevant details, which can be sent out with the invitation.

For advice on alternative gift lists – such as asking for money, vouchers or even the honeymoon – log on to www.confetti.co.uk/giftlists

Information packs

It's not unusual these days to cross the Atlantic for a family wedding. Friends and family who come from overseas to share your special day are likely to be planning a holiday around it. To help them make the most of their trip, you could consider sending them information details containing local travel details, accommodation and tourist information. It shouldn't cost you more than a few pennies either, as all the information can be simply presented on a single sheet of A4 and posted with your wedding invitation.

Your information pack should include :

Directions and maps

Send guests travel information well in advance, especially if they need to book air or rail tickets. Tips about the nearest airport or cheapest way to obtain tickets will be welcome. The numbers of local taxi firms may also prove invaluable. Remember, out-of-town guests may not have a car available to them: it's a nice thought to arrange for a coach or minibus to pick them up from the hotel and take them to the ceremony venue, and then on to the reception.

Accommodation cards

Many hotels will allow block reservations of rooms, as long as they are confirmed by a certain date. This usually enables you to negotiate a more favourable rate, especially during the off-peak season. Otherwise, you could send them details and phone numbers of local bed and breakfasts. Make sure you include as many as possible, as there will always be someone who leaves it till the last minute, and you don't want them phoning you up in a panic because they can't find anywhere to stay!

Example

A room will be provided for you at:
[venue name, address and phone number].
Please make reservations before [date and month].

Guests who have travelled a fair distance only to be faced with the predicament of trying to find somewhere nice to eat at the end of a long and tiring day will truly appreciate a list of addresses and numbers of local restaurants where they can go and revive themselves!

Tourist information

If you live near Stonehenge or Snowdon, Brighton Pavilion or Blackpool Pleasure Gardens, include some tourist leaflets with your information pack, or leave them in your guests' rooms for their arrival.

Other inclusions

Reply card (see page 13).
Ceremony card (see page 58).
Admission card (see page 59).

A note about information packs

Although you can print your information on plain A4 paper, there is no traditional etiquette here; coordinating your information pack with your invitations will, however, certainly look more impressive and exciting. This doesn't need to be too complex.

Here are some ideas:

- Use the same typeface as on your invitations.
- Print on a good-quality cream or ivory paper, or use a colour to coordinate with your invitations.
- Bind with a ribbon in the same colour as your invitations.
- Lay the information out on the page as attractively as possible, and don't try to cram too much in.
- If you're photocopying, always photocopy from the original – however it's preferable to print out each copy separately.

Order of service sheets

The advantage of order of service sheets is that the
congregation can follow the service without having to
juggle with hymn and prayer books. The printer will probably
have a sample layout on which your individual requirements
can be based.

An order of service usually takes the form of a folded card,
with or without a paper insert. The cover of the sheet will
traditionally have the names of the bride and groom printed
in the bottom left- and right-hand corners respectively. The
date and the name of the church in which the service is to
take place will be centred in the middle of the page. The
layout of the service sheet will depend on the style of the
ceremony, and couples should ensure their chosen elements
of the service have been approved by their minister before
making final arrangements for printing.

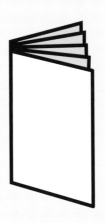

It is always sensible to have a few extra order of service sheets printed for unexpected guests. Make sure you include the minister, choir and attendants when calculating the number required.

Example
(cover)

> name of church
> location
> the marriage of
> [bride]
> &
> [groom]
> [date and time]

(inside)
entrance music for bride
introduction
hymn
the marriage
prayers (optional)
reading (optional)
blessing (optional)
hymn
reading/blessing (optional)
signing of the register
exit music

Gift acknowledgment cards

Thank you cards are discussed in more detail on pages 108–115. If the newlyweds are planning to go on an extended honeymoon, they may wish to send gift acknowledgment cards. These are a polite way of thanking guests for their gifts before the thank you cards are sent.

Gift acknowledgment cards may also be sent when there is a large volume of thank you cards that might take some time to write. Sending a simple acknowledgment initially will allow you more time to write personalized thank you cards later on.

Example

Mr & Mrs [first name and surname]
have received your very kind gift
and will contact you later with their thanks.

After the wedding

With more and more guests travelling long distances and staying overnight, it's becoming common practice for parents or the bride and groom themselves to host an informal brunch at their house or a local pub the next day. Often invitations are informal and by word of mouth, but you could also mention the brunch in your information pack (see pages 68–70) or use the following wording:

Mr and Mrs [host names]
invite you to brunch
following their marriage/the marriage of their
daughter/son/the marriage of [name] and [name]
on [day and date]
at [time]
at [venue + full address]

Wedding announcements

Traditionally, wedding announcements are made by the bride's parents, and are sent to family and friends who were not invited to the wedding. They should always be sent after the wedding has taken place, never before; any time up to a year after is acceptable.

The announcements should follow the same format as the wedding invitations, and should be engraved in black ink on white or ecru-coloured letter sheets.

The bride's parents have 'the honour of announcing' or have 'the honour to announce' is the usual form of wording. It is acceptable to simply 'announce the marriage of their daughter' for less formal announcements, though this could be construed as the bride's parents disapproving of their new son-in-law.

As announcements are sent after the event, the year should be included, written in words ('two thousand and four'), with the name of the church or venue below.

It is perfectly acceptable for wedding announcements to be sent by the bride and groom.

Example

Mr and Mrs [bride's parents' names]
have the pleasure of announcing
the marriage of their daughter
[bride's name]
to
Mr [groom's name]
[day and date]
[year in words]
[venue + full address]

The wedding ceremony itself is by no means the only ceremony involved in weddings.

A blessing is a short ceremony that takes place after the official marriage ritual: normally after a civil wedding, as a religious ceremony generally includes the blessing as a matter of course. After some years, couples may like to re-affirm their vows to each other. Although for some couples this is a low-key affair, some like to involve family and friends in a large, formal celebration.

Blessings

Separate invitations would not normally be sent, as the order of events on the day would consist of a ceremony, blessing and reception. If space is limited, however, you may wish to invite guests to just the blessing and ceremony.

Example

Mr & Mrs Wakefield
request the honour of your presence
at a blessing and ceremony for their daughter
Laura-Jayne Elizabeth
and Adam Steven Austin
on [day, month, year]
at [time]
at
St George's Church, Barton-in-Fabis,
Nottingham

Renewal of vows

Not all couples, by any means, choose to reaffirm their wedding vows, but many – particularly those married in civil ceremonies – may wish to do so in order to include a religious element in their marriage.

Just like the wedding invitation, these invitations should be formal in their style.

Example

> Mr and Mrs [married couple's names]
> request the honour of your presence
> at a ceremony to celebrate
> the renewal of their wedding vows
> on [day and date]
> at [time]
> at [venue + full address]

Recently, some local authorities have started offering renewal of vows ceremonies. If you arrange to have such a ceremony in a register office, you may want to add another line to the invitation:

> And afterwards at a reception/dinner/party
> at [venue + full address]

Thanksgiving for Marriage

The Thanksgiving for Marriage service is a Church of England ceremony.

Example

Mr and Mrs [married couple's names]
request the honour of your presence
at a
Thanksgiving for Marriage
on [day and date]
at [time]
at [venue + full address]

Event invitations

Formal dinner parties may be held for a specific occasion, such as a birthday, or they may be in honour of a particular guest or event, such as a family member graduating from university or getting a new job.

Example

In honour of
Fiona French,
Mr and Mrs John Rogers
request the pleasure of your company
at dinner
on [day and date]
at [time]
at [venue + full address]

Or

To mark the Little Hovering Cricket XI
Golden Jubilee,
The Captain and his wife
request the pleasure of your company
at dinner
on [day and date]
at [time]
at [venue + full address]
RSVP

It is common practice to state two times, for example 'seven-thirty for eight'. This indicates that cocktails will precede the dinner, which will be served at the later time.

Lunches

These are very similar to dinner invitations but are almost always hosted only by the lady of the house. Again, they are often held to honour a special guest, milestone or achievement. Traditionally, when the lady of the house hosts an event, she is known by her married title – Mrs Louise Haworth, or even Mrs John Haworth. If the hostess has not taken her husband's name, then she should not use a title.

Example

Louise Franklin
requests the pleasure of your company
on [day and date]
at [time]
at [venue + full address]

'At Home'

An 'At Home' invitation is sent from the lady of the house and indicates a non-dining social event such as a drinks party or afternoon tea.

An 'At Home' event usually has a start and end time, and guests can arrive at any time during that period.

Example

Mrs Louise Haworth
At Home
date [in full]
from [time] to [time]
address
RSVP (this is not strictly necessary)

16th birthday

In North America, a Sweet Sixteen is the first big birthday party of a girl's adult life, and the idea is catching on over here. As with all modern celebrations, there are no hard and fast rules, but here's an example of the wording you might use.

Example (from the parents)

Fiona Millar
is celebrating her
Sweet Sixteen Birthday.
Let's help her celebrate
on [day and date]
at [time]
at [venue + full address]

RSVP Tom and Rebecca Millar
[contact details]

Or

Please be our guest as we celebrate the Sweet Sixteen of
[girl's name]

Example (from the birthday girl)

A girl turns Sweet Sixteen only once in her life,
Please join me to celebrate this special occasion.

18th birthday

An 18th birthday party is held to mark a child's entry into adulthood. Traditionally, the key to the door is given to symbolize the gaining of freedom.

Example

Mr & Mrs [parents' names]
request the pleasure of your company
to celebrate their daughter
[girl's name]
coming of age
on [day and date]
at [time]
at [venue + full address]
Dress code: Black tie
RSVP

Or

[Birthday boy's name]
is having an 18th birthday party
on [day and date]
at [time]
at [venue + full address]
RSVP

21st birthday

It's usual to throw a party to celebrate turning 21. Invitations to birthday parties don't have to be formal unless the event is a formal affair, such as a black tie event.

Example

Mr & Mrs [parents' names]
request the pleasure of your company
to celebrate their daughter
[name]
coming of age
on [day and date]
at [time]
at [venue + full address]
Dress code: Black tie
RSVP

Or

You are cordially invited
to a dinner
for [name]
to celebrate his/her 21st birthday
on [day and date]
at [time]
at [venue + full address]
RSVP

30th birthday

Turning 30 is a real milestone for most people, a point in their lives when they assess how far they've come, so celebrating your 30th is a must! Invitations can be as formal or as informal as the occasion.

Example

I'm turning 30!
Please join me in waving goodbye to my 20s
at a BBQ at my place on
on [day and date]
at [time]
at [venue + full address]

40th birthday

Life begins at 40, so they say! And what better excuse to throw a party? Invitations to birthday parties don't have to be formal unless the event is a formal affair, such as a black tie event.

Example

[First name and surname]
requests the pleasure of your company
for cocktails and dancing
to celebrate
my 40th birthday!
on [day and date]
at [time]
at [venue + full address]
RSVP

60th birthday

There are lots of things to celebrate when you turn 60, and free bus travel is just one of them! You're probably at a time in your life when you are more settled than ever, you have a family and possibly even grandchildren too – so throw a party!

Example

[First name and surname]
requests the pleasure of your company
to celebrate
his/her 60th birthday
on [day and date]
at [time]
at [venue + full address]
RSVP

100th birthday

The Queen sends out congratulatory messages to British citizens at home and abroad on their 100th birthday. If you wish to commemorate a centenary with this greeting, see page 93 for more details.

Cocktail parties

Like an 'At Home' invitation (see page 85), a cocktail party invitation indicates that no formal dinner will be served, although it is usual to serve canapés or even a light buffet.

Stating 'cocktail party' on your invitation is an excellent way to convey to your guests that they should make other dinner plans – there are few things more inconvenient for a guest than not knowing whether food will be served during an evening get-together. Cocktail parties are usually held early in the evening.

Example

Laura and Peter Cockroft
invite you for cocktails
on [day and date]
at [time]
at [venue + full address]

Anniversaries

Wedding anniversaries are traditionally celebrated in association with a material of some kind. These start from paper, representing the first anniversary, to platinum representing 75 years; the materials become increasingly precious with the passing of the years. Although the earlier anniversaries tend to be celebrated *à deux*, the 25th, 40th, 50th and 60th anniversaries, in particular, are often celebrated with big family parties.

The Queen sends out congratulatory messages to British citizens at home and abroad on their 60th, 65th and 70th anniversaries, and each one thereafter.

To ensure someone you know receives a message from the Queen, you need to complete a form and send it no more than three weeks before the anniversary date to:
The Anniversaries Office
Buckingham Palace
London SW1A 1AA

You can download the form from the internet at
www.royalinsight.gov.uk/output/Page546.asp

Read *Anniversaries and Celebrations*, also in this series, for more advice and ideas.

Anniversary parties are often hosted by a couple's children or friends, in their honour.

Example

[Host or hosts' name(s) and surname(s)]
request(s) the pleasure of your company
at an Anniversary Party
in honour of
[couple's names]
on [day and date]
at [time]
at [venue + full address]
RSVP [phone number]   Silver/Gold/Platinum

Example

Mr and Mrs [host's names]
request the pleasure of your company
at a dinner to celebrate
the 50th wedding anniversary
of
Mr and Mrs [couple's names]
on [day and date]
at [time]
at [venue + full address]
RSVP

Couples celebrating wedding anniversaries may well prefer charitable donations to be made instead of receiving gifts. You can indicate this on the invitation by adding a comment in the lower right-hand corner, such as:

Gifts to the Furry Friends Cat Home

Baby showers

The baby shower is an American tradition that is fast gaining popularity on this side of the Atlantic. It usually involves only the mother-to-be and female friends and, like wedding showers, is hosted by friends, not family.

Example

Fiona French
cordially invites you
to a baby shower
in honour of
Lesley Ann Moore
on [day and date]
at [time]
at [venue + full address]
RSVP

Sometimes these are surprise events:

Example

You are cordially invited
to a surprise baby shower
in honour of
Lesley Ann Moore
on [day and date]
at [time]
at [venue + full address]
RSVP Fiona French [contact details]

Christenings/Namings

These invitations need to go out only about a month before the event. For more details on both christenings and naming ceremonies, see www.confetti.co.uk/parties

Example (Christening)

We request the honour of your presence at
the baptism of
[baby's name]
on [day and date]
at [time]
at [venue + full address]
RSVP [parents' names and address]

Or

[Parents' names] have been blessed.
Please join us at the Christening of
[baby's name]
on [day and date]
at [time]
at [venue + full address]
Followed by drinks
at [venue + full address]
RSVP

Offering a real civil alternative to Christenings, naming ceremonies are on the rise.

Example (naming)

> You are invited to join in the happiness of
> [parents' names]
> in celebrating the birth of
> [baby's name]
> on [day and date]
> at [time]
> at [venue + full address]
> RSVP

Or

> [Parents' names] invite you to celebrate
> the birth and naming of
> [baby's name]
> on [day and date]
> at [time]
> at [venue + full address]
> RSVP

Children's parties

The wording for children's parties is almost always informal, especially when the guests are too young to understand what 'requests the pleasure of your company' means! To assist parents, it's best to be as clear as possible on the invitation about what kind of party it will be. It's also common to include the time that the party will end, to indicate when children should be picked up.

Example

[Name of child] is having a pool party
from (start time) to [end time]
[day, date, venue + full address]
Towels will be provided.

Or

You are invited to [name of child's] Bowling Party
from [start time] to [end time]
[day, date, venue + full address]

Or

[Name of child] and Barbie
invite you to a dressing-up party
from [start time] to [end time]
[day, date, venue + full address]

For more information on children's parties, see www.confetti.co.uk/parties

Bar/Bat Mitzvah

There is no standard etiquette for a Bar or Bat Mitzvah invitation, but such an occasion is a religious one and celebrates the attainment of religious maturity, so the tone and wording should be in keeping with the formality of the occasion.

Example

Mr and Mrs Benjamin Cohen
cordially invite you to worship with them
on the occasion of the
Bar Mitzvah of their son
Samuel
on [day and date]
at [time]
at [name of temple + full address]
The service will be followed by lunch.

Surprise parties

A 'surprise party' is one where the guest of honour does not
know that there will be a party. These are most commonly
held for birthdays or anniversaries. When inviting guests to
a surprise party, in addition to the usual details of date,
location, time, etc. It is important to convey that the guest of
honour must be kept in the dark about the arrangements.
Alternatively include a note saying 'Surprise Party'.

Example

Surprise Party!
In honour of Caroline Morrow's 30th Birthday
[venue + full address]
[day and date]
at [time]
RSVP Rachel Browne/Lily Hall

Or

Peter and Jane Latchford
request the pleasure of your company
at a surprise dinner
to celebrate the 50th anniversary of Peter's parents
Ernest and Barbara
on [day and date]
at [time]
at [venue + full address]
Your discretion is appreciated!

For more tips on how to throw a successful surprise party,
read, *Anniversaries and Celebrations* also in this series.

Cards & announcements

In this section, we cover a variety of occasions when you might find it necessary to send a written greeting or announcement.

One example, changing your name, most commonly takes place after marriage, when the bride adopts the groom's surname, or the bride and groom double-barrel their surnames. The bride's children by a previous marriage may adopt the groom's surname.

Another common name change is when a divorced woman reverts to her maiden name.

Example (bride taking groom's surname)
Fiona Finch
is delighted to announce
that on the occasion of her marriage to John Wilson
she will now be known as
Fiona Wilson

Example (bride and groom adopting a double-barrelled surname)
Fiona Finch and John Wilson
announce that on the occasion of their marriage
they will take the surname/family name of
Wilson-Finch

Example (bride's children adopting a double-barrelled surname)
On the occasion of the marriage
of their mother Fiona
to John Wilson,
Charlie, Peter and Amy Brown
will now be known as
Charlie, Peter and Amy Wilson-Finch

Example (reverting to a maiden name)
Mrs Fiona Wilson
announces that she will resume the use
of her maiden name
and will now be known as
Ms Fiona Finch

Change of address

These are normally very straightforward, but again can be made more informal. There are different texts for notifications sent before and after a change of address.

Example (before the move)

From [date]
our new address will be
[new address]
[new address]
[new telephone number]

Fiona and John Wilson-Finch

Example (after the move)

Fiona and John Wilson-Finch
[new address]
[new address]
[new telephone number]

Birth announcement

There is a wide choice of ways to word these
announcements, from the very simple and formal
to the more informative.

Example

Chloe Grace Wilson
August the Seventh, 2004
7lb 6oz

Mr and Mrs John Wilson

Or

Mr and Mrs John Wilson
announce the birth of their daughter
Chloe Grace
August the Seventh,
Two Thousand and Four
7lb 6oz

If the parents have different surnames, then the child's full name should be stated:

Example

It's a boy!

Joshua James Wilson-Finch
Born to
John Wilson &
Fiona Finch
[date]

Thank you cards

Your guests may have spent a considerable amount of time and money on a carefully chosen gift for you. It is good manners, therefore, to send each contributor a card or letter thanking them for their kindness and thoughtfulness.

Unfortunately, letter writing is a dying art and many people have had little practice at thanking people for gifts by letter. In fact, most see it as a chore to be endured in childhood at the end of birthday and Christmas celebrations. This need not be the case.

It's best if your thank you cards are ordered to match your invitations and other stationery. If you don't have thank you stationery to match your invitations, invest in some quality heavyweight writing paper or cards. Many stationers, including the Confetti stores, now stock a range of writing materials at reasonable prices.

How to phrase a thank you note

These usually consist of four or five parts, depending on whether the gift-giver was present at your event or not.

The first part is the greeting, which should be polite but informal: regardless of how formal your invitations may have been, it is not appropriate to start a thank you note with 'Dear Admiral and Lady Worthington' or 'Dear Dr and Mrs Brand'.

Then move on to the thanks. It is always best to mention the gift specifically. Writing 'Thank you for your thoughtful gift' is a dead giveaway that you have no clue what the gift was, for example:

'Thank you for the stunning Tiffany vase.'

'How thoughtful of you to give us the butter dish.'

'We can't thank you enough for the beautiful cutlery.'

Follow this up with a comment on how the gift will add to your life, for example:

'It's already in pride of place in the dining room.'

'I'm sure it has already made our toast taste better in the mornings!'

'I can't believe how beautiful the umbrella is – I'm almost wishing that it would rain so I can use it!'

If the gift-giver came to your party or wedding, mention something about your appreciation of their presence on the day, for example:

'We were so thrilled everyone was there to share our day with us.'

'I hope you've recovered from my grandmother's impromptu Madonna impression.'

'Thanks so much for coming all the way from Timbuktu for the dinner – I really appreciate it.'

And, finally, express your hope that you will see or talk to the gift-giver in the near future, for example:

'Let's meet up when you are next in town.'

'I hope you'll come and stay soon (and use the butter dish!).'

'Please come and see us – enjoying our new lamp – soon!'

Thank you notes for weddings

The question most often asked about thank you letters is whether to send thank you letters on receipt of the gifts or wait until after the honeymoon.

The answer is that you should write your thank you letters as soon as you receive your gifts (or when you have been notified by the store you are using for your wedding list that a gift has been purchased for you). Writing immediately upon receipt acknowledges the safe arrival of the gift. It also means that you write a few letters a week, rather than having the full task to come back to at the end of your honeymoon.

Thank you cards for gifts that arrive very close to your wedding day, or on the day itself, should be written as soon as you return from your honeymoon. These letters can take a different form, as you will be able to reminisce about the wonderful day you both enjoyed. People who were unable to attend your wedding may also purchase gifts: a note written after your wedding will give you the opportunity to tell them how everything went, as well as possibly including a wedding photograph.

Your thank you notes should be handwritten, though it is perfectly acceptable to have cards printed with a message of thanks that you add to. Traditionally, thank you letters are written by the bride, but there is no reason why the task should not be shared. After all, the gift is for both of you. Make sure you have a record of who gave what; this is easy to do if most of your gifts came via a store wedding list service, as most stores record the givers' names on their print-out.

Saying thank you for money

If you have been given money, do not mention the amount, but say what use you will be putting it to. The giver will be pleased to know that their money has been put to good use in your home.

Example

Dear Michelle and David,
Just a note to thank you for your generous wedding gift. It has been duly deposited in our savings account, which is earmarked for our dining-room suite.
    We have now chosen the colour scheme for the room, so the pleasure of choosing our furniture is not far away. Funny how quickly you get used to eating from a tray in the lounge – the cats love it!
    You must come round once we are totally decorated and organized.
Love,
Beth & John

Belated thank you notes

Sending belated thank you notes some time after an event or
after a gift has been received is fine, as long as you include an
apology for its lateness. It is also usual to give a reason, for
example, you were ill and unable to send a card earlier.

Example

Dear Jane,
Just a short note to thank you for your very kind [gift],
which arrived last month. I am sorry that I was not able
to write sooner, but I have been on holiday for three
weeks and found your parcel waiting for me at home.
I was feeling quite down about leaving all that sun and
sand behind, so it was fantastic to find a present waiting
for me on my return!
Looking forward to meeting up soon,
Beth

Thank you notes for parties

Sending a thank you note to the host after a party is a lovely gesture and one that they are bound to appreciate. Thank you notes can be as formal or as informal as you wish, though it is best to send thanks as soon after an event as possible.

If you would like to send thanks to hosts after a wedding to which you received a formal invitation, it is usual to send a formal thank you. Don't forget that they will also be sending you a thank you card for your gift! When writing thank you notes, try to write as you would speak. You might like to include an anecdote from the event – perhaps a comment you heard from one of the guests, a mention of a guest you were introduced to and with whom you got on particularly well, or a funny story about something you saw.

Camera cards

Disposable cameras are now almost indispensable at every gathering, but it's useful to put notes with the cameras in order to remind guests to use them and to leave them for you to develop at the end of the evening!

Camera cards such as these are now available preprinted from an event stationer such as Confetti, or you can write them yourself. They can be plain or coordinate with the rest of your stationery. The text can be kept simple:

Example

> Please use the camera to capture
> some memories of our special day.
>
> Leave the used camera on the table
> for us to collect later.

However, some people prefer to leave something a little more creative, and camera poems are now much in vogue. Here is a selection of some basic rhymes.

Example

To celebrate this special day,
Pick a camera and really play.
Leave it on the table when you are done,
We'll develop the photos and share the fun!

Or

I'm your camera – so have some fun,
You'll make our album a special one.
Snap away as best you're able,
Then drop me off at the gift table!

Or

This camera's provided so
We'll have pictures of people we know.
Take snaps if you're able
Of friends on your table
And leave it behind when you go!

Or

Take this camera and have some fun
Get some pictures of everyone!
We hope you'll take something we didn't see
That we can keep as a memory!

Electronic etiquette for invitations

Beautifully designed and printed invitations are exciting to receive, and set the tone for the entire event. Whether formal or casual, traditional or contemporary, the invitation says more about the event than can be expressed in words. But in a nation of texters and emailers, has it become acceptable to send invitations electronically?

In a recent poll, a quarter of Confetti users said they wouldn't be offended at receiving a wedding invitation by text or email. However, this carried a certain number of conditions. People said they would still like to receive a formal written invitation as a follow-up. It's also worth noting that if you are going to invite some guests by email or text message, you should invite them all through this medium. If hosts send proper invitations to some guests and electronic messages to others, feelings could get very hurt.

There are a number of websites that enable hosts to invite guests to parties via ecard, and then the guests reply to the website, creating an automatic guest list. If you are sending invitations by post but still wish to use an online guest list, try www.confetti.co.uk

Replying to invitations by email or text

If the hosts have gone to a great deal of trouble to include a special reply card with your invitation, it's only good manners to use it to RSVP. However, spending time contacting people who haven't replied to invitations is one of the biggest problems for party organizers in the precious last weeks before the event. If the only way you will get round to replying without being prompted is to send an email or text message, then by all means do so – it's much better than not replying at all.

Chasing RSVPs via email or text

Confetti Agony Aunt and wedding expert Aunt Betti receives many queries each year from brides wanting to know the etiquette for following up guests who haven't replied by the required date. 'Email and text are an absolute gift here,' she says. 'When you're busy finalizing your plans, it's much easier to send a quick email than to spend your evenings phoning round, hoping you catch people at a convenient moment.'

Thanking guests via email or text

Just as we still prefer to receive Christmas or birthday cards rather than emails, so it's always best to thank your guests for gifts with a handwritten card or letter. All too often emails or text messages can seem as though no thought has been put into them – which is definitely the wrong message to send!

Stationery tips & information

With the amount of junk mail and brown envelopes that come through the letterbox every day, the appearance of your invitation or thank you card, in a stylish envelope, individually addressed, is even more essential.

Don't leave addressing your envelopes to the last minute. After spending so much time on selecting your stationery and compiling inserts, you don't want to spoil the whole effect by rushing your envelopes. Leave at least a month for events with larger guest lists, and make sure you have absolutely everyone's full address.

Strictly speaking, printed labels or envelopes are not appropriate. However, the style of your invitations and envelopes may lend themselves to printed labels. Generally, though, handwritten envelopes provide the finishing touch to the whole package.

You might like to hire a calligrapher to write the envelope for a truly professional look, but you can also invest in a calligraphy pen and practise first if you are confident enough. Traditionally, envelopes should be addressed in black ink to match the invitations. If your invitations are printed in another colour, you may like to match this instead.

Addressing the envelope

When a guest receives a correctly and formally addressed envelope, it immediately signals that you have put a lot of thought into the invitation and, by extension, the event. There are two parts to this: the name and the address.

The name

The guests' names should be written in full on the outer envelope. Don't use nicknames or initials, and use appropriate social titles. A married couple will be addressed as 'Mr and Mrs James Thornton'. A married couple where the woman has retained her maiden name should be addressed 'Mary Philips and Roger Tracey'. Although it is correct to say 'Dr and Mrs' it is not correct to say 'Dr and Mr'. This should be amended to Dr Anne Grey and Mr Thomas Grey'. In general, if the couple both have different professional titles, the woman should be listed first, and first names should be in full.

The address

Always write out addresses in full, for example, 219 Trinity Street, rather than 219 Trinity St. Don't abbreviate place or county names: write Hampshire, not Hants.

The finishing touches

Confetti

When 'stuffing' your envelopes, add a small handful of coordinating confetti. This will fall out when the guest opens the invitation and create a celebratory feel.

Wax seals

These are an old-fashioned touch which is becoming more popular, especially on wedding invitations. A block of specialist sealing wax (note: not a domestic candle!) is melted onto the fold of the envelope, and then stamped. Stamps are widely available in pre-designed bells, hearts and doves, and also made-to-order initials.

Inner and outer envelopes

Formal wedding invitations are sent in two envelopes, a tradition from when they were delivered by hand. The outer envelope bearing the address would be opened by the footman, and the inner envelope, would be handed to the household. Nowadays, this means that whatever state your outer envelope arrives in, the inner one should still be in pristine condition.

It's nice to know how to address a formal invitation envelope properly, even if you decide not to send them out. Your guests' names and addresses should appear on the outer envelope, while their names alone, in the form of title and surname, should appear on the inner envelope. The rear flap of the outer envelope has only the sender's address, engraved or blind-embossed on it.

Social stationery

As well as the different kinds of stationery outlined in this book, the good host or hostess will have a selection of stationery ready for any correspondence that may arise.

This may include:

Letterhead paper

This is paper printed with the writer's name (without titles or academic letters) and address at the top of the page. It is most commonly printed in black ink on white or ivory paper, and can be either embossed or engraved. In embossing the ink is slightly raised from the page, and in engraving it is slightly recessed into it. This paper is suitable for longer missives or more formal correspondence.

Monogrammed notes

These are small notes, with matching (plain) envelopes. The writer's embossed monogram (a combination of your initials) appears at the top. These can be more brightly coloured than letterheads, and are useful for sending thank you notes or replying to invitations.

Printing and copyright

When it comes to the printing of the wedding stationery, many couples are concerned about the vexed issue of copyright. Most couples who marry in church will choose to have two or three hymns and a non-religious reading, and they will want to detail these for their guests in the order of service. Music for civil weddings may be more modern, but couples will still wish to provide details of each song and its author.

Copyright exists in creative works such as hymns, poems and prayers for 70 years after the death of the writer. During that period, it is illegal to reproduce the works in any form without the permission of the copyright holder (or their appointed agent). Should you wish to reproduce the text of a hymn in your order of service, you will need the permission of the copyright holder, for which a charge of between £10 and £25 is usually made. You will find details of the copyright holder at the bottom of the page on which the hymn is originally printed. But remember, many hymns are out of copyright because of their age, and you do not need the copyright holder's permission if you are only singing the hymns, since a wedding is a private function.

If this all sounds a little daunting, don't worry – if you order your invitations and stationery through Confetti, we'll take care of the copyright issue for you!

INDEX

Confetti.co.uk is the UK's leading weddings and special occasion website, helping more than 400,000 brides, grooms and guests every month.

Confetti.co.uk is packed full of ideas and advice to help organize every stage of your wedding. At Confetti, you can choose from hundreds of beautiful wedding dresses; investigate our list of more than 3,000 wedding and reception venues; plan your wedding; chat to other brides about their experiences and ask for advice from Aunt Betti our agony aunt. If your guests are online, too, we will even help you set up a wedding website to share details and photos with your family and friends.

Our extensive online content on every aspect of weddings and special occasions is now complemented by our range of books covering every aspect of planning a wedding, for everyone involved. Titles include the complete *Wedding Planner*; *Getting Married Abroad*; *How to Write a Wedding Speech*; *The Best Man's Speech*; *Jokes, Toasts and One-liners for Wedding Speeches*; *Wedding Readings and Vows*; *Wedding Dresses*; *The Bride's Wedding*; *The Groom's Wedding*; *The Father of the Bride's Wedding*; *Your Daughter's Wedding* and *Men at Weddings*.

Confetti also offer:
Wedding & special occasion stationery – our stunning ranges include all the pieces you will need for all occasions, including christenings, namings, anniversaries and birthday parties.
Wedding & party products – stocking everything you need from streamers to candles to cameras to cards to flowers to fireworks and, of course, confetti!

To find out more or to order your confetti gift book, party brochure or wedding stationery brochure, visit: www.confetti.co.uk call: 0870 840 6060; email: info@confetti.co.uk
visit: Confetti, 80 Tottenham Court Road, London W1T 4TE
or Confetti, The Light, The Headrow, Leeds LS1 8TL